Praying the Psalms
with the Holy Fathers

Compiled by Peter Celano

PARACLETE PRESS
BREWSTER, MASSACHUSETTS

Praying the Psalms with the Holy Fathers

2011 First Printing

Copyright © 2011 by Paraclete Press, Inc.

ISBN: 978-1-55725-777-2

Library of Congress Cataloging-in-Publication Data

Praying the Psalms with the Holy Fathers / edited by Peter Celano.
   p. cm.
  Includes indexes.
  ISBN 978-1-55725-777-2
  1. Bible. O.T. Psalms—Meditations. 2. Catholic Church—Prayers and devotions. I. Celano, Peter.
  BS1430.54.P69 2011
  242'.5—dc22

                     2010046750

10 9 8 7 6 5 4 3 2 1

Published by Paraclete Press
Brewster, Massachusetts
www.paracletepress.com

Printed in the United States of America

CONTENTS

PART II
REFLECTIONS
ON FAVORITE PSALMS

INTRODUCTION

OVER THE LAST TWO THOUSAND YEARS, the best guides to the beauty and spirituality of the book of Psalms have been the Holy Fathers. Popes, past and present, have delivered homilies full of quotations from the Psalms, written special messages to the faithful explaining the meaning of various psalms, and most important, have made praying the psalms a part of their own spiritual lives and practices.

The book of Psalms is the greatest spiritual poetry in the history of literature. You may be familiar with the words of certain psalms from your own prayer life, or from the liturgy of the Mass, when we pray at least a portion of a psalm each week. Holy Fathers have prayed these beautiful, universal words for millennia. Like King David himself (the author of nearly half of the psalms), who cared for sheep before his unlikely battle with the giant Goliath, the Holy Fathers can shepherd us through the wisdom of these graceful texts.

Two thousand years ago, St. Peter would have prayed the Psalms in Hebrew, the language in which they were originally written. Jesus and the disciples also prayed them in Hebrew in the first century AD.

Pope Gregory the Great prayed the psalms in the Latin of the Middle Ages. For centuries, various popes insisted that the Psalms, like all of Holy Scripture, should not be translated from the Latin. Pope Innocent III, for instance, forbade their translation into French in 1199, believing that vernacular copies of the Bible could be easily misunderstood by the people. But times changed, and today the Psalms are sung, prayed, spoken, heard, felt (there are many excellent Braille editions), and read in many languages all over the world.

Pope John Paul II grew up praying the Psalms in his native Polish. In fact, Pope John Paul "the Great" was a great lover of these prayer poems, having given a long series of Wednesday audiences dedicated to explaining the prayers of the Divine Office for morning and evening. He died before he was able to finish these audiences devoted exclusively to exploring and explaining the Psalms.

Our current Pope, Benedict XVI, grew up praying these powerful words in both German and the Latin of the church.

Of course many a pope has also prayed them in Italian!

The book of Psalms is a collection of 150 poem-prayers that were originally written as religious songs. Some of them are even handed down to us with suggestions for instrumental accompaniment. For instance, take a look at Psalm 54 in your own Bible. Before the first verse, you probably see something like this:

For the choirmaster On stringed instruments.

You will notice similar instructions before other psalms. You will also notice superscriptions such as the one before Psalm 22:

For the choirmaster To "the Doe of the Dawn"
Psalm of David

There are various theories of where these instructions originated. One was perhaps an ancient reference to a deer that David had encountered while he was out in the fields, and it had inspired him in the writing of those verses. We don't know for sure. The Psalms are full of mystery as well as music.

In the oldest manuscripts seventy-three of these prayer songs are attributed to David. Tradition has it that David was often writing (and singing) words that were based on earlier (but no longer extant) songs of figures such as Adam and Moses. Wouldn't it be intriguing if David was repeating some of what had been passed down by oral tradition for centuries? In any case, these verses are truly ancient in origin, predating all of the writings in the New Testament. Some of them were surely sung in the First Temple—the one built by King Solomon, David's son—from about 800 to 750 BC.

In any language, time, or place, the poetry of the Psalms sings to our souls. One of the most familiar and beloved passages of them all, Psalm 23:1–3, reads like this in one familiar English translation:

The Lord is my shepherd, I shall not want.
He makes me lie down in green pastures;
he leads me beside still waters;
he restores my soul.
He leads me in right paths for his name's sake.

In any language, the words of the psalmist speak to our hearts and deepest desires.

Taken together, the psalms represent many things to our spiritual lives:

- They speak to God from the depths of human experience and emotion.
- They tell of the desires, fears, and loves of the Jewish people—in ways that are universal of the desires, fears, and loves of all people everywhere.
- They express hope for the Messiah that was to come, and will come again.
- They understand the silence we often feel in the presence of God.
- And they show, too, the human desire to speak—sometimes, even shout or weep—in God's holy presence.

The book of Psalms was as popular two thousand years ago as it is now. The writers of the New Testament Scriptures knew this Hebrew poetry. There are various places in the New Testament where specific psalms are mentioned. We also know that Jesus was steeped in the Psalms. For instance, on one occasion, while talking with the Pharisees, Jesus refers to David's words in the Psalms in order to explain to the Pharisees the meaning and identity of the Messiah (see Matthew 22:41–46). Jesus prayed psalms in the temple, talked about them in the temple, and prayed them at home. The Psalms were a part of his religious formation, as they were for every Jewish child.

Praying the Psalms with the Holy Fathers offers you an opportunity to discover this portion of Scripture for yourself, perhaps for the first time. It also gives you the opportunity to learn from these songs that have fed the souls of our Hebrew forebears, of our Lord, and of all Christians since the time of the first disciples.

⁓

The personalities of the popes vary greatly. Each pope has his own way of communicating, and each his unique messages for the essential life of the church in his day. This collection follows in the tradition of two books previously published by Paraclete Press: *Christmas with the Holy Fathers* (2008) and *Lent and Easter with the Holy Fathers* (2010). As was the case in those books, this one also includes messages from Holy Fathers going back in history as far as Pope St. Leo the Great (AD 440–61). This collection would be weak if it did not include the reflections of Pope Leo. Pope Benedict XVI said, at one of his weekly Wednesday audiences, that Pope Leo "was one of the greatest incumbents of the See of Rome, the authority and prestige of which he strengthened. He is also the earliest pope whose sermons have come down to us, sermons he would address to the people who gathered around him during celebrations."

But while this collection of reflections includes Holy Fathers as ancient as Pope St. Leo the Great, it also includes Holy Fathers as recent as Pope Benedict XVI and his immediate predecessor, Pope John Paul II (1978–2005). In his very first papal message from the loggia of St. Peter's Basilica, Benedict XVI referred to John Paul II as "the great" and since that time, Christians all over the world have been calling him Pope John Paul the Great, waiting for the day to come soon when they might add "saint" before his name.

The words that follow are for all Christians everywhere—in fact, all people who desire to know the will of God for their lives today. The messages of the popes are vital for the people of God—not just for Roman Catholics. In every era, the Holy Father speaks to the world, and the world listens to what he has to say.

Before we read the words of the Holy Fathers about specific psalms, let us conclude this introduction with the words of Pope St. Pius X on his own experience with the Psalms.

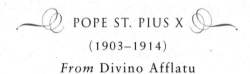 POPE ST. PIUS X

(1903–1914)

From Divino Afflatu

*It is good to give thanks to the Lord, to sing praises to your
name, O Most High.*

PSALM 92:1

THE COLLECTION OF PSALMS found in Scripture, composed as it was under divine inspiration, has, from the very beginnings of the Church, shown a wonderful power of fostering devotion among Christians as they offer to God a continuous sacrifice of praise, the harvest of lips blessing his name.

The Psalms seem to me to be like a mirror, in which the person using them can see himself, and the stirrings of his own heart; he can recite them against the background of his own emotions. Augustine says in his *Confessions:* "How I wept when I heard your hymns and canticles, being deeply moved by the sweet singing of your Church. Those voices flowed into my ears, truth filtered into my heart, and from

14

my heart surged waves of devotion. Tears ran down, and I was happy in my tears."

Who can fail to be moved by those many passages in the psalms which set forth so profoundly the infinite majesty of God, his omnipotence, his justice and goodness and clemency, too deep for words, and all the other infinite qualities of his that deserve our praise? Who could fail to be roused to the same emotions by the prayers of thanksgiving to God for blessings received, by the petitions, so humble and confident, for blessings still awaited, by the cries of a soul in sorrow for sin committed? Who would not be fired with love as he looks on the likeness of Christ, the redeemer, here so lovingly foretold? His was the voice Augustine heard in every psalm, the voice of praise, of suffering, of joyful expectation, of present distress.

PART I
MAJOR THEMES

Foretelling the Coming of Christ

INTRODUCTION

THE COMING OF CHRIST was foretold by the Hebrew prophets over and over again in what Christians call the Old Testament. As one example, this statement from the eleventh chapter of the book of Isaiah was later repeated in the first verse of the first Gospel of the New Testament. In both passages the message is clear: the Messiah will come from the root of Jesse's (David's) family tree.

A shoot shall come out from the stump of Jesse, and a branch shall grow out of his roots. . . . On that day the root of Jesse shall stand as a signal to the peoples; the nations shall inquire of him, and his dwelling shall be glorious. (Isaiah 11:1, 10)

An account of the genealogy of Jesus the Messiah, the son of David, the son of Abraham. . . . So all the generations from Abraham to David are fourteen generations; and from David to the deportation to Babylon, fourteen generations; and from the deportation to Babylon to the Messiah, fourteen generations. (Matthew. 1:1, 17)

Jesse was the father of King David, and there is direct genealogical line from David to Jesus, as Matthew explains in chapter one of his Gospel. The first Christians understood this connection between David and Jesus intimately; they often spoke of it.

For example, in Acts four, the disciples Peter and John were imprisoned because they had been preaching about the risen Christ. When they were released, Peter and John

raised their voices together to God and said: "Sovereign Lord, who made the heaven and the earth, the sea, and everything in them, it is you who said by the Holy Spirit through our ancestor David, your servant: 'Why did the Gentiles rage, and the peoples imagine vain things? The kings of the earth took their stand, and the rulers have gathered together against the Lord and against his Messiah.' For in this city, in fact, both Herod and Pontius Pilate, with the Gentiles and the peoples of Israel, gathered together against your holy servant Jesus, whom you anointed." (vv. 23–27)

This connection from King David to Jesus Christ is one of the reasons Christians have always felt a close connection to the words of David. Nowhere are David's words (and spirit) better preserved than in the book of Psalms. One interesting tradition among some of the early monastics is that the incarnate Christ was the one who inspired David in the actual writing of the Psalms. This comes from the unusual phrase that begins Psalm 110: "The Lord says to my lord . . ." (v. 1).

In this first section of *Praying the Psalms with the Holy Fathers*, we see David's words expressing the hope and expectation of the Jewish people for the coming of the Messiah. We see psalms that foretell the coming of Christ.

The Glorious Figure of the Messiah King

POPE JOHN PAUL II

Meditation on Psalm 72, December 2004

For he delivers the needy when they call,
  the poor and those who have no helper.
He has pity on the weak and the needy,
  and saves the lives of the needy.
From oppression and violence he redeems their life;
  and precious is their blood in his sight.

Long may he live!
  May gold of Sheba be given to him.
May prayer be made for him continually,
  and blessings invoked for him all day long.
May there be abundance of grain in the land;
  may it wave on the tops of the mountains;
  may its fruit be like Lebanon;
and may people blossom in the cities
  like the grass of the field.
May his name endure for ever,
  his fame continue as long as the sun.
May all nations be blessed in him;
  may they pronounce him happy.
            PSALM 72:12–17

THE CHRISTIAN TRADITION HAS seen in this image of the Messiah and King a foreshadowing of Jesus Christ, Son of the Virgin Mary, the long-awaited Savior.

According to a characteristic of messianic poems, the whole of nature is involved in a transformation which is first of all social: The wheat of the harvest will be so abundant as to become almost like a sea of ears of wheat waving on the top of the mountains (see v. 16). It is the sign of divine blessing that pours itself out in fullness on a pacified and serene earth. What is more, the whole of humanity, letting fall and canceling every division, will converge toward this sovereign of justice, thus fulfilling the great promise made by the Lord to Abraham: "May all nations be blessed in him" (v. 17; see Genesis 12:3).

In his "Commentary on Psalm 71," St. Augustine, re-reading the song precisely in a Christological vein, explained that the indigent and the poor whom Christ comes to rescue are "the people of believers in him." Recalling the kings mentioned earlier in the Psalm, he specifies that "in this people are included also the kings who adore him. They have not, in fact, disdained to be indigent and poor, that is, to humbly confess their sins and recognize themselves in need of the glory and grace of God, so that that king, son of the king, would free them from the powerful one," namely Satan, the slanderer, the strong one. "But our Savior humiliated the slanderer, and entered the house of the strong one, snatching his riches from him after chaining him; he freed the indigent one from the powerful one, and the poor one who had no one to save him." This, in fact, could not have been done by any created power: not that of a just man or that of an angel. "There was no one able to save us; that is why he came, in person, and has saved us."

The Magi's Gifts Offered by All Who Come to Christ

POPE ST. LEO THE GREAT

Letter to the bishops of Sicily

May all kings fall down before him,
all nations give him service.

PSALM 72:11

THIS DAY, ON WHICH CHRIST the Savior of the world first appeared to the nations, must be venerated by us with holy worship. Today those joys must be entertained in our hearts which existed in the breasts of the three magi. Aroused by the sign and leading of a new star, which they believed to have been promised, they fell down in the presence of the King of heaven and earth. That day has not passed away; the mighty work, which was then revealed, hasn't passed away with it. We don't only celebrate the report of something that once happened.

By the oft-repeated gift of God, we daily enjoy the fruit of what the first age possessed. And therefore, although the narrative which is read to us from the Gospel properly records those days on which the three men, who had neither been taught by the prophets'

25

predictions nor instructed by the testimony of the law, came to acknowledge God from the furthest parts of the East, yet we behold this same thing more clearly and abundantly now in the enlightenment of all who are called. The prophecy of Isaiah is fulfilled when he says, "the Lord has laid bare His holy arm in the sight of all the nations, and all the nations upon earth have seen the salvation which is from the Lord our God." And again, "and those to whom it has not been announced about Him shall see, and they who have not heard, shall understand."

So when we see people devoted to worldly wisdom and far from belief in Jesus Christ brought out of the depth of their error and called to an acknowledgment of the true Light, it's undoubtedly the brightness of the Divine grace that is at work. And whatever new light illumines the darkness of their hearts comes from the rays of the same star: so that it should both move with wonder, and going before lead to the adoration of God the minds which it visited with its splendor.

Do you wish to see how the magi's three gifts may also be offered by all who come to Christ with the foot of faith? The same offering is repeated in the hearts of true believers. For he that acknowledges Christ the King of the universe brings gold from the treasure of his heart: he that believes the Only-begotten of God to have united man's true nature to Himself, offers myrrh; and he that confesses Him as being in no wise inferior to the Father's majesty, worships Him in a manner with incense.

POPE ST. GREGORY
THE GREAT
(c. 540–604)

From his Commentary on Job, *Book IV*

> *Yet he, being compassionate,*
>   *forgave their iniquity,*
>   *and did not destroy them;*
> *often he restrained his anger,*
>   *and did not stir up all his wrath.*
> *He remembered that they were but flesh,*
>   *a wind that passes and does not come again.*

PSALM 78:38–39

ALMIGHTY GOD WAS ABLE to create good things out of nothing, so that when he was ready, he restored the good things that were lost by the mystery of his Incarnation. At first, he made two creations to contemplate himself—the angelic and the human— but pride ruined them both and dashed them from their original, native uprightness. One of them had the clothing of flesh, while the other bore no infirmity derived from flesh. (For an angelic being is spirit alone, while man is both spirit and flesh.) Therefore

28

when the Creator took compassion to work redemption, it was good that he should bring back to himself that creature, which, in the commission of sin, plainly still held on to some infirmity. And it was also good that the apostate Angel should be driven down to a farther depth, in proportion, so that when he fell from resoluteness in standing fast, he carried about himself no infirmity of the flesh.

It is in all of this that the psalmist tells of the Redeemer's compassion for humankind in these words: "He remembered that they were but flesh" (Psalm 78:39). It's as if he said, "God beheld their infirmities so that he wouldn't punish their offences with severity." It is like this that humankind is brought to the light of repentance by the coming of the Redeemer.

Long Ago David Sang of the Coming of Christ

From a homily on The Feast of the Epiphany

A Prayer of David.
  Incline your ear, O LORD, and answer me,
    for I am poor and needy.
 Preserve my life, for I am devoted to you;
    save your servant who trusts in you.
You are my God; be gracious to me, O LORD,
    for to you do I cry all day long.
Gladden the soul of your servant,
    for to you, O LORD, I lift up my soul.
 For you, O LORD, are good and forgiving,
    abounding in steadfast love to all who call on you.
Give ear, O LORD, to my prayer;
    listen to my cry of supplication.
 In the day of my trouble I call on you,
    for you will answer me.

There is none like you among the gods, O LORD,
    nor are there any works like yours.
All the nations you have made shall come
    and bow down before you, O LORD,
    and shall glorify your name.
 For you are great and do wondrous things;
    you alone are God.
 Teach me your way, O LORD,
    that I may walk in your truth;
    give me an undivided heart to revere your name.

I give thanks to you, O LORD my God, with
*   my whole heart,*
*   and I will glorify your name for ever.*
For great is your steadfast love towards me;
*   you have delivered my soul from the depths of Sheol.*

O God, the insolent rise up against me;
*   a band of ruffians seeks my life,*
*   and they do not set you before them.*
But you, O LORD, are a God merciful and gracious,
*   slow to anger and abounding in steadfast love*
*   and faithfulness.*
Turn to me and be gracious to me;
*   give your strength to your servant;*
*   save the child of your serving-maid.*
Show me a sign of your favor,
*   so that those who hate me may see it and be put to shame,*
*   because you, LORD, have helped me and*
*   comforted me.*

PSALM 86

LET'S JOYFULLY CELEBRATE the day of our first-fruits and the commencement of the nations' calling: "giving thanks to the merciful God who made us worthy," as the Apostle says, "to be partakers of the lot of the saints in light: who delivered us from the power of darkness and translated us into the kingdom of the Son of His love." As Isaiah prophesied, "the people of the nations that sat in darkness have seen a great light, and they that dwelt in the land of the shadow of death, upon them hath the light shined." He also said to the Lord, "nations which did not know thee, shall call on thee: and people that were ignorant of thee, shall run together unto thee." It was on this day that "Abraham saw and was glad," when he understood that the sons of his faith would be blessed in his seed, that is in Christ, and foresaw that by believing he should be the father of all nations.

It is this day that David sang of in the psalms saying, "All the nations you have made shall come and bow down before you, O Lord, and shall glorify your name" (Psalm 86:9).

And again, David said: "The Lord has made known his victory: he has revealed his vindication in the sight of the nations" (Psalm 98:2).

This we know to have taken place ever since the three wise men aroused in their far-off land were led by a star to recognize and worship the King of heaven and earth. And their worship of Him exhorts us to imitation; that, as far as we can, we should serve our gracious God who invites us all to Christ. In which regard, we ought to all help one another, so that in the kingdom of God, which is reached by right faith and good works, we may shine as the sons of light: through our Lord Jesus Christ, Who with God the Father and the Holy Spirit lives and reigns forever and ever. Amen.

All Creation Sings!

[L]et the field exult, and everything in it.
Then shall all the trees of the forest sing for joy.

PSALM 96:12

Let the floods clap their hands;
let the hills sing together for joy.

PSALM 98:8

THIS IS EMMANUEL, GOD-WITH-US, who comes to fill the Earth with grace. He comes into the world in order to transform creation. He becomes a man among men, so that in him and through him every human being can be profoundly renewed. By his birth, he draws us all into the sphere of the divine, granting to those who in faith open themselves to receiving his gift, the possibility of sharing in his divine life.

This is the meaning of the salvation which the shepherds hear proclaimed that night in Bethlehem: "To you is born a Savior" (Luke 2:11). The coming of Christ among us is the center of history, which thereafter takes on a new dimension. In a way, it is God himself who writes history by entering into it. The event of the Incarnation thus broadens to embrace the whole of human history, from creation until the Second Coming. This is why in the Liturgy all creation sings, voicing its own joy: "The floods clap their hands, all the trees of the world sing for joy, and the many coastlands are glad" (see Psalms 98:8, 96:12; 97:1).

Every creature on the face of the Earth receives the proclamation. In the astonished silence of the universe, the words which the Liturgy puts on the lips on the Church take on a cosmic resonance: *Christus natus est nobis. Venite, adoremus!*

Christ is born for us. Come let us adore him.

The Messiah Will Triumph

POPE JOHN PAUL II
General Audience, November 26, 2003

The LORD says to my lord,
  "Sit at my right hand
until I make your enemies your footstool."

The LORD sends out from Zion
  your mighty scepter.
  Rule in the midst of your foes.
Your people will offer themselves willingly
  on the day you lead your forces
  on the holy mountains.
  From the womb of the morning,
  like dew, your youth will come to you.
The LORD has sworn and will not change his mind,
  "You are a priest for ever according to the order of
Melchizedek."

PSALM 110:1-4

BROTHERS AND SISTERS, each Sunday at Evening
Prayer the Church celebrates Christ's resurrection by
chanting Psalm 110. The Psalm, originally composed

for the enthronement of an earthly King born of the line of David, celebrates the final victory of the Messiah over all his enemies. By a solemn divine oath, the King is also made "a priest for ever according to the order of Melchizedek." The Church reads this Psalm as a pre-figuration of the enthronement of Jesus Christ, our King and High Priest, at the right hand of the Father. From his heavenly throne the Risen Lord invites us to contemplate the glory to which we are called as members of his Mystical Body.

Psalms of Repentance

INTRODUCTION

THE MOST FAMILIAR AND POPULAR prayer for
Catholics today is most likely the Rosary. However,
Jesus never prayed the Rosary. It didn't exist in those
days. Instead, Jesus prayed the psalms every day. He
and the disciples likely prayed most of the Psalter (a
book containing only the Psalms) from memory. As
a boy, Jesus would have begun to learn the psalms
in detail in the synagogue. Every devout Jew prayed
them daily.

The influence of the psalmists' words permeates all
of Jesus' teachings. In fact, it was Martin Luther who
once called the Psalms "the Lord's Prayer in miniature,"
because of how the themes of that most famous and
repeated prayer of Jesus reverberates with the poetry
of the Psalms. If for no other reason, these are the
reasons why we would be blessed to know the Psalms
better than we do.

Throughout the Gospels, we see incidents of
Jesus at prayer—during the events of the Passion we
see Jesus turning again and again to their familiar
phrases.

From the cross, our Lord said:

"My God, my God, why have you forsaken me?"
PSALM 22:1A

And as his final breath, he uttered:

Into your hand I commit my spirit.
PSALM 31:5A

The following selections emphasize how our Lord prayed the psalms, and how they can be for us a profound religious language for sin, repentance, and forgiveness.

⌒

Seven Penitential Psalms

SEVEN SPECIAL PSALMS have been called "the penitentials" since at least the sixth century. St. Augustine of Hippo referred to four of them and in doing so used that term even one hundred years earlier. Pope Innocent III was the first Holy Father to ask that these seven psalms be prayed every year during the season of Lent. They are beloved of Christians for the way in which they communicate the spirit of our Lord.

The words of these special psalms are often the topic of Ash Wednesday homilies. It is during Holy Week that we focus most of all on these songs of the church.

The penitential psalms are the truest subject and the sincerest material for any soul who desires to practice Lenten spirituality. In these words, we encounter the spirit of Jesus as he prayed with the disciples, as he spent time alone in the desert, while he prayed and wept in the Garden of Gethsemane, and in his final moments on the cross.

As Pope Benedict XVI said in his homily for Ash Wednesday in 2006:

A new heart and a new spirit: we ask for this with the penitential Psalm par excellence. . . . The true believer, aware of being a sinner, aspires with his whole self—spirit, heart and body—to Divine forgiveness, as to a new creation that can restore joy and hope to him.

It was once common for Catholics to observe multiple "Lents" throughout the year. Perhaps we should revive this practice once again. Allow these words—of the spirituality of our Lord—to begin to form you more deeply in the coming days.

A TRADITIONAL PRAYER FOR SINCERE REPENTANCE

PSALM 6

O LORD, do not rebuke me in your anger,
or discipline me in your wrath.
Be gracious to me, O LORD, for I am languishing;
O LORD, heal me, for my bones are shaking
with terror.
My soul also is struck with terror,
while you, O LORD—how long?

vv. 1–3

MOST HUMANE AND LOVING LORD, Your endless grace and mercy overwhelm me. Before granting the gift of absolution to earnest repenters of sinful ways, You demanded a sacrificial compensation. For a wrongful act cannot be rectified until punishment has been accepted. Yes, for the salvation of my very soul, You accepted the price of Your very Son, Jesus Christ, on the Cross! I pray You, grant me the grace to remain free of trespasses, so that my heart might remain flawless before You, making Your absolution truly worthwhile!

40

POPE JOHN PAUL II
General Audience, May 19, 2004

Happy are those whose transgression is forgiven,
whose sin is covered.
Happy are those to whom the LORD imputes no iniquity,
and in whose spirit there is no deceit.

While I kept silence, my body wasted away
through my groaning all day long.
For day and night your hand was heavy upon me;
my strength was dried up as by the heat of
summer.
Then I acknowledged my sin to you,
and I did not hide my iniquity;
I said, "I will confess my transgressions to the
LORD,"
and you forgave the guilt of my sin.

vv. 1–5

"HAPPY IS THE MAN whose offence is forgiven, whose sin is remitted"! This beatitude that opens Psalm 32 allows us to understand immediately why it was welcomed by Christian tradition into the series of the seven penitential Psalms. Following the introductory twofold beatitude, we do not discover a generic reflection on sin and forgiveness, but the personal witness of one who has converted.

Above all, the person praying describes his very distressful state of conscience by keeping it "secret" (v. 3): having committed grave offences, he did not have the courage to confess his sins to God. It was a terrible interior torment, described with very strong images. His bones waste away, as if consumed by a parching fever; thirst saps his energy and he finds himself fading, his groan constant. The sinner felt God's hand weighing upon him, aware as he was that God is not indifferent to the evil committed by his creature, since he is the guardian of justice and truth.

Unable to hold out any longer, the sinner made the decision to confess his sin with a courageous declaration that seems a prelude to that of the prodigal son in Jesus' parable (see Luke 15:18). Indeed, he said with a sincere heart: "I will confess my offence to the Lord." The words are few but born from conscience: God replies immediately to them with generous forgiveness (v. 5).

The prophet Jeremiah made this appeal to God: "Return, faithless Israel, says the Lord. I will not look on you in anger, for I am merciful, says the Lord. I will not be angry forever. Only acknowledge your guilt, that you rebelled against the Lord your God" (Jeremiah 3:12–13).

A PENITENTIAL RITE

O LORD, do not rebuke me in your anger,
*   or discipline me in your wrath.*
For your arrows have sunk into me,
*   and your hand has come down on me.*

There is no soundness in my flesh
*   because of your indignation;*
there is no health in my bones
*   because of my sin.*
For my iniquities have gone over my head;
they weigh like a burden too heavy for me.

My wounds grow foul and fester
*   because of my foolishness.*

vv. 1–5

IT IS FROM THE PENITENTIAL PSALMS that the "Penitential Rite" comes, as we recite in Mass each week. There are different versions of this, and each one picks up on the themes of these seven psalms of David.

Priest: You raise the dead to life in the Spirit:
   Lord, have mercy.

All: Lord, have mercy.

Priest: You bring pardon and peace to the
   sinner: Christ, have mercy.

All: Christ, have mercy.

Priest: You bring light to those in darkness:
   Lord, have mercy.

All: Lord, have mercy.

Priest: May almighty God have mercy on
   us, forgive us our sins, and bring us to
   everlasting life.

All: Amen.

POPE JOHN PAUL II

General Audience, July 30, 2003

> *Have mercy on me, O God,*
>   *according to your steadfast love;*
> *according to your abundant mercy*
>   *blot out my transgressions.*
> *Wash me thoroughly from my iniquity,*
>   *and cleanse me from my sin.*

vv. 1–2

WE HEAR PROCLAIMED PSALM 51, the famous *Miserere.* Indeed, it is presented anew to us on the Friday of every week, so that it may become an oasis of meditation in which we can discover the evil that lurks in the conscience and beg the Lord for purification and forgiveness. Indeed, as the Psalmist confesses in another supplication, "O Lord . . . no man living is righteous before you" (Psalm 143:2). In the Book of Job we read: "How can man be righteous before God? How can he who is born of woman be clean? Behold, even the moon is not bright, and the stars are not clean in his sight; how much less man, who is a maggot, and the son of man, who is a worm!" (25:4–6).

These are strong, dramatic words that are intended to portray the full seriousness and gravity of the limitations and frailty of the human creature, his perverse capacity to sow evil and violence, impurity and falsehood. However, the message of hope of the *Miserere* which the Psalter puts on the lips of David, a converted sinner, is this: God can "blot out, wash and cleanse" the sin confessed with a contrite heart. The Lord says, through the voice of Isaiah, even if "your sins are scarlet, they shall be as white as snow; though they are red like crimson, they shall become like wool" (Isaiah 1:18).

POPE BENEDICT XVI
General Audience, October 19, 2005

Out of the depths I cry to you, O Lord.

Lord, hear my voice! Let your ears be attentive to the voice of my supplications!

If you, O Lord, should mark iniquities, Lord, who could stand?

But there is forgiveness with you, so that you may be revered.

I wait for the Lord, my soul waits, and in his word I hope;

my soul waits for the Lord more than those who watch for the morning, more than those who watch for the morning.

vv. 1–6

ONE OF THE PSALMS best-known and best-loved in Christian tradition has just been proclaimed: the *De profundis*, as it was called from its beginning in the Latin version. With the *Miserere*, it has become one of the favorite penitential Psalms of popular devotion.

Over and above its use at funerals, the text is first and foremost a hymn to divine mercy and to the reconciliation between the sinner and the Lord, a

God who is just but always prepared to show himself "a merciful and gracious God, slow to anger and rich in kindness and fidelity, continuing his kindness for a thousand generations, and forgiving wickedness and crime and sin" (Exodus 34:6–7).

For this very reason, our Psalm is inserted into the liturgy of Vespers for Christmas and for the whole Octave of Christmas, as well as in the liturgy of the Fourth Sunday of Easter and of the Solemnity of the Annunciation.

Psalm 130 opens with a voice that rises from the depths of evil and sin (vv. 1–2). The person who is praying addresses the Lord in the first person: "I cry to you, O Lord." The Psalm then develops in three parts, dedicated to the subject of sin and forgiveness. The Psalmist first of all addresses God directly, using the *Tu*: "If *you*, O Lord, should mark our guilt, Lord, who would survive? But with you is found forgiveness: for this we revere you" (vv. 3–4).

It is significant that reverent awe, a sentiment in which respect and love are mingled, is not born from punishment but from forgiveness. Rather than sparking his anger, God's generous and disarming magnanimity must kindle in us a holy reverence. Indeed, God is not an inexorable sovereign who condemns the guilty but a loving father whom we must love, not for fear of punishment, but for his kindness, quick to forgive.

POPE JOHN PAUL II

General Audience, July 9, 2003

Hear my prayer, O Lord; give ear to my supplications
in your faithfulness;
answer me in your righteousness.
Do not enter into judgment with your servant, for no
one living is righteous before you.

vv. 1–2

THE LAST OF THE SO-CALLED "Penitential Psalms."
. . . The Christian tradition has used all of them to
seek pardon from God for its sins. The text that we
want to examine today was particularly dear to St.
Paul, who detected in it a radical sinfulness of every
human creature: "for no man living is righteous before
you, (O Lord)" (v. 2). This thought is used by the
Apostle as the foundation of his teaching on sin and
grace (see Galatians 2:16 and Romans 3:20).

The Psalm begins with an intense and insistent
invocation directed to God, faithful to his promise
of salvation offered to the people (v. 1). The person
in prayer recognizes his unworthiness and therefore
humbly asks God not to act as a judge (v. 2).

Then he traces a dramatic situation, similar to an earthly nightmare, which he is battling; the enemy, who represents evil in history and in the world, has led him to the threshold of death. He has fallen, in fact, into the dust of the earth, which is probably an image of the grave; then there is the darkness which is the absence of the light, a divine sign of life; then finally, "the deaths of great time," that is, the long-gone dead (v. 3), among which he seems to be already relegated.

The Psalmist's very being is devastated: he cannot even breathe and his heart seems like a piece of ice, incapable of continuing to fight (v. 4). To the faithful, knocked down and trampled, only the hands are left free, which stretch towards the sky in a gesture that is, at the same time, one of imploring help and seeking assistance (v. 6). The thought, in fact, recalls the past when God wrought marvels (v. 5).

This spark of hope warms the ice of suffering and the test in which the person in prayer feels immersed and at the point of being swept away (v. 7). The tension, however, remains ever strong; but a ray of light seems to appear on the horizon.

PART II
REFLECTIONS
ON FAVORITE PSALMS

INTRODUCTION

THE HOLY FATHERS HAVE OFTEN selected the
Psalms for extended reflections on matters of faith.
It has been said that all of the Bible might be contained in the Psalter—which means that every issue
of our faith and life, and every theological topic, is
addressed in these songs to God.

What follows is a selection of some of these
longer reflections from the Holy Fathers on specific
psalms throughout history. The psalms selected for
inclusion here represent some of the favorite psalms
of Christians down through the ages.

In addition, many of the most important teachings
of the Holy Fathers in regard to particular psalms
come in the midst of a homily or address on a broader
topic. For example, in the middle of an encyclical "On
Health and Apostolic Benediction," Pope John XXIII
said this about a brief but important passage from
Psalm 135 (that is also picked up in Psalm 115:2–4):

> Your name, O LORD, endures forever, your
> renown,
>   O LORD, throughout all ages.

> For the LORD will vindicate his people, and have
> compassion on his servants.
> The idols of the nations are silver and gold,
> the work of human hands.

PSALM 135:13–15

Speaking to all the citizens of the world, the "Good Pope" (that's what his fellow Italians lovingly nick-named John XXIII) had this to say:

> Our Predecessor, Pius XII, rightly asserted that our age is marked by a clear contrast between the immense scientific and technical progress and the fearful human decline shown by "its monstrous masterpiece . . . transforming man into a giant of the physical world at the expense of his spirit, which is reduced to that of a pygmy in the supernatural and eternal world."
>
> And so the words of the psalmist about the worshippers of false gods are strikingly verified today. Men are losing their own identity in their works, which they admire to the point of idolatry: "The idols of the nations are silver and gold, the work of human hands."

In Our paternal care as universal Pastor of souls, We earnestly beg Our sons, immersed though they be in the business of this world, not to allow their consciences to sleep; not to lose sight of the true hierarchy of values.

And so, you will also find some shorter reflections here.

POPE JOHN XXIII

From *the encyclical* Pacem in Terris

How Majestic Is Your Name

O LORD, *our Sovereign,*
  how majestic is your name in all the earth!

PSALM 8:1A

PEACE ON EARTH, WHICH ALL men of every era have most eagerly yearned for, can be firmly established only if the order laid down by God be dutifully observed. The progress of learning and the inventions of technology clearly show that, both in living things and in the forces of nature, an astonishing order reigns, and they also bear witness to the greatness of man, who can understand that order and create suitable instruments to harness those forces of nature and use them to his benefit. But the progress of science and the inventions of technology show above all the infinite greatness of God, Who created the universe and man himself. He created all things out of nothing, pouring into them the abundance of His wisdom and goodness, so that the holy psalmist praises God in these words: "O Lord, our Sovereign, how majestic is your name in all the earth!"

POPE JOHN PAUL II

General Audience, January 30, 2002

God Creates the Brilliance of the Sun

To the leader. A Psalm of David.
The heavens are telling the glory of God;
*   and the firmament proclaims his handiwork.*
Day to day pours forth speech,
*   and night to night declares knowledge.*
There is no speech, nor are there words;
*   their voice is not heard;*
yet their voice goes out through all the earth,
*   and their words to the end of the world.*

In the heavens he has set a tent for the sun,
which comes out like a bridegroom from his wedding
*   canopy,*
*   and like a strong man runs its course with joy.*
Its rising is from the end of the heavens,
*   and its circuit to the end of them;*
*   and nothing is hidden from its heat.*

The law of the LORD is perfect,
      reviving the soul;
the decrees of the LORD are sure,
      making wise the simple;
the precepts of the LORD are right,
      rejoicing the heart;
the commandment of the LORD is clear,
      enlightening the eyes;
the fear of the LORD is pure,
      enduring for ever;
the ordinances of the LORD are true
      and righteous altogether.
More to be desired are they than gold,
      even much fine gold;
sweeter also than honey,
       and drippings of the honeycomb.

Moreover by them is your servant warned;
      in keeping them there is great reward.
But who can detect their errors?
      Clear me from hidden faults.
Keep back your servant also from the insolent
      do not let them have dominion over me.
Then I shall be blameless,
      and innocent of great transgression.

Let the words of my mouth and the meditation
  of my heart
  be acceptable to you,
O Lord, my rock and my redeemer.

THE SUN, WITH ITS INCREASING brilliance in the heavens, the splendor of its light, the beneficial warmth of its rays, has captivated humanity from the outset. In many ways human beings have shown their gratitude for this source of life and well-being, with an enthusiasm that often reaches the peaks of true poetry. The wonderful psalm, 18, whose first part has just been proclaimed, is not only a prayerful hymn of extraordinary intensity; it is also a poetic song addressed to the sun and its radiance on the face of the earth. In this way the Psalmist joins the long series of bards of the ancient Near East, who exalted the day star that shines in the heavens, and which in their regions dominates with its burning heat. It reminds us of the famous hymn to Aton, composed by the Pharoah Akhnaton in the 14th century BC and dedicated to the solar disc regarded as a deity.

But for the man of the Bible there is a radical difference in regard to these hymns to the sun: The sun is not a god but a creature at the service of the one God and Creator. It is enough to think of the words of Genesis: "God said, 'Let there be lights in the firmament of the heavens to separate the day from the night; and let them be for signs and for seasons and for days and years. . . . God made the two great lights, the greater light to rule the day, and the lesser light to rule the night. . . . And God saw that it was good.'"

Before examining the verses of the Psalm, let us take a look at it as a whole. Psalm 18 is like a diptych: in the first part (vv. 1–6) we find a hymn to the Creator, whose mysterious greatness is manifest in the sun and in the moon. In the second part of the Psalm (vv. 7–14), instead, we find a sapiential hymn to the *Torah*, the Law of God. A common theme runs through both parts: God lights the world with the brilliance of the sun and illuminates humanity with the splendor of his word contained in biblical Revelation. It is almost like a double sun: the first is a cosmic epiphany of the Creator; the second is a free and historical manifestation of God our Savior. It is not by chance that the Torah, the divine Word, is described with solar features: "The commandment of the Lord is pure, enlightening the eyes" (v. 8).

63

But let us now examine the first part of the Psalm. It begins with a wonderful personification of the heavens, that to the sacred author appear as eloquent witnesses to the creative work of God (vv. 1–4). Indeed, they narrate or proclaim the marvels of the divine work. Day and night are also portrayed as messengers that transmit the great news of creation. Their witness is a silent one, but makes itself forcefully felt, like a voice that resounds throughout the cosmos.

With the interior gaze of the soul, men and women can discover that the world is not dumb but speaks of the Creator when their interior spiritual vision, their religious intuition, is not taken up with superficiality. As the ancient sage says: "from the greatness and beauty of created things their original author is seen by analogy" (Wisdom 13:5). St. Paul, too, reminds the Romans that "ever since the creation of the world, [God's] invisible perfections can be perceived with the intellect in the works that have been made by him" (Romans 1:20).

The hymn then yields place to the sun. The shining globe is depicted by the inspired poet as a warrior hero who emerges from the marital chamber where he spent the night, that is, he comes forth from the heart of darkness and begins his unwearying course through the heavens. The sun is compared to an athlete, who does not know rest or fatigue, while our entire planet is enveloped in its irresistible warmth.

So the sun is compared to a bridegroom, a hero, a champion, who, by divine command, must perform a daily task, a conquest and a race in the starry spaces. And here the Psalmist points to the sun, blazing in the open sky, while the whole earth is wrapped in its heat, the air is still, no point of the horizon can escape its light.

The solar imagery of the Psalm is taken up by the Christian liturgy of Easter to describe Christ's triumphant exodus from the dark tomb and his entry into the fullness of the new life of the Resurrection. At Matins for Holy Saturday, the Byzantine liturgy sings: "As the sun rises after the night in the dazzling brightness of renewed light, so you also, O Word, will shine with new brightness, when after death, you leave your nuptial bed." An Ode for Matins of Easter links the cosmic revelation with the Easter event of Christ: "Let the heavens rejoice and the earth exult with them because the whole universe, visible and invisible, takes part in the feast: Christ, our everlasting joy, is risen." And another Ode adds: "Today the whole universe, heaven, earth, and abyss, is full of light and the entire creation sings the resurrection of Christ our strength and our joy." Finally, another concludes: "Christ our Passover is risen from the tomb like a sun of justice shining upon all of us with the splendor of his charity."

The Roman liturgy is not as explicit as the Eastern in comparing Christ to the sun. Yet it describes the cosmic repercussions of his Resurrection, when it begins the chant of Lauds on Easter morning with the famous hymn: *Aurora lucis rutilat, caelum resultat laudibus, mundus exultans iubilat, gemens infernus ululate*—"The dawn has spread her crimson rays, And heaven rings with shouts of praise; The glad earth shouts her triumph high, And groaning hell makes wild reply."

The Christian interpretation of the Psalm, however, does not invalidate its basic message, that is an invitation to discover the divine word present in creation. As stated in the second half of the Psalm, there is another and more exalted Word, more precious than light itself, that of biblical Revelation. For those who have attentive ears and open eyes, creation is like a first revelation that has its own eloquent language: it is almost another sacred book whose letters are represented by the multitude of created things present in the universe. St. John Chrysostom says: "The silence of the heavens is a voice that resounds louder than a trumpet blast: this voice cries out to our eyes and not to our ears, the greatness of Him who made them." And St. Athanasius says: "The firmament with its magnificence, its beauty, its order, is an admirable preacher of its Maker, whose eloquence fills the universe."

POPE BENEDICT XVI

April 9, 2009

The Good Shepherd Lays Down His Life

> *The LORD is my shepherd, I shall not want.*
>> *He makes me lie down in green pastures;*
> *he leads me beside still waters;*
>> *he restores my soul.*
> *He leads me in right paths*
>> *for his name's sake.*
>
> *You prepare a table before me*
>> *in the presence of my enemies;*
> *you anoint my head with oil;*
>> *my cup overflows.*

PSALM 23:1–3, 5

AFTER THE BREAD, JESUS TAKES the chalice
of wine. The Roman Canon describes the chalice
which the Lord gives to his disciples as *praeclarus calix*
("the glorious cup"), thereby alluding to Psalm 23, the
Psalm which speaks of God as the Good Shepherd,
the strong Shepherd. There we read these words:

"You have prepared a banquet for me in the sight of my foes . . . My cup is overflowing"—*calix praeclarus*. The Roman Canon interprets this passage from the Psalm as a prophecy that is fulfilled in the Eucharist: yes, the Lord does indeed prepare a banquet for us in the midst of the threats of this world, and he gives us the glorious chalice—the chalice of great joy, of the true feast, for which we all long—the chalice filled with the wine of his love. The chalice signifies the wedding-feast: now the "hour" has come to which the wedding feast of Cana had mysteriously alluded. Yes indeed, the Eucharist is more than a meal; it is a wedding feast. And this wedding is rooted in God's gift of himself even to death. In the words of Jesus at the Last Supper and in the Church's Canon, the solemn mystery of the wedding is concealed under the expression *novum Testamentum*. This chalice is the new Testament—"the new Covenant in my blood," as Saint Paul presents the words of Jesus over the chalice (1 Corinthians 11:25). The Roman Canon adds: "of the new and everlasting covenant," in order to express the indissolubility of God's nuptial bond with humanity. The reason why older translations of the Bible do not say Covenant, but Testament, lies in the fact that this is no mere contract between two parties on the same level, but it brings into play the infinite distance between God and man. What we call the new and the ancient Covenant is not an agreement between two equal parties, but simply the gift of God who bequeaths to us his love—himself. Certainly, through this gift of his love, he transcends all distance and makes us truly his "partners"—the nuptial mystery of love is accomplished.

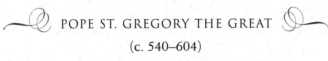

POPE ST. GREGORY THE GREAT
(c. 540–604)

From his Commentary on Job, *Book IV*

Prove Me, O Lord

> *Prove me, O LORD, and try me;*
> *test my heart and mind.*
>
> PSALM 26:2

WE SHOULD MARK HOW THE LORD lets go of our enemy, and yet, keeps him reigned in—how God looses and yet bridles him. God allows him some things for temptation, but withholds him from others. . . . For whenever many bad tidings fall on our shoulders, by the wonderful graciousness of the Creator they are measured out in seasons; if they came all at once they would destroy us.

It's for this reason that St. Paul says, God is faithful, "No testing has overtaken you that is not common to everyone. God is faithful, and he will not let you be tested beyond your strength, but with the testing he will also provide the way out so that you may be able to endure it" (1 Corinthians 10:13). And David says,

"Prove me, O Lord, and try me" (Psalm 26:2). It's as if David said in plainer words, "First examine my powers, and then, as I am able to bear, let me undergo temptation."

POPE JOHN PAUL II

General Audience, June 13, 2001

The Lord Solemnly Proclaims His Word

Ascribe to the LORD, O heavenly beings,
  ascribe to the LORD glory and strength.
Ascribe to the LORD the glory of his name;
  worship the LORD in holy splendor.

The voice of the LORD is over the waters;
  the God of glory thunders,
  the LORD, over mighty waters.
The voice of the LORD is powerful;
  the voice of the LORD is full of majesty.

The voice of the LORD breaks the cedars;
  the LORD breaks the cedars of Lebanon.
He makes Lebanon skip like a calf,
  and Sirion like a young wild ox.

The voice of the LORD flashes forth flames of fire.
The voice of the LORD shakes the wilderness;
  the LORD shakes the wilderness of Kadesh.

The voice of the LORD causes the oaks to whirl,
  and strips the forest bare;
  and in his temple all say, "Glory!"

The LORD sits enthroned over the flood;
  the LORD sits enthroned as king for ever.
May the LORD give strength to his people!
  May the LORD bless his people with peace!

PSALM 29

SOME EXPERTS CONSIDER Psalm 29 as one of the most ancient texts of the Psalter. A powerful image unifies it in its poetic and prayerful unfolding: in fact, we face the progressive unleashing of a storm. The Hebrew term *qol*, which signifies both "voice" and "thunder," repeated at the beginning of key verses creates the mounting tension of the psalm. For this reason commentators call our Psalm the "Psalm of seven thunders," for the number of times in which the word resounds. In fact, one can say that the Psalmist thinks of thunder as a symbol of the divine voice, with its transcendent and unattainable mystery, that breaks into created reality in order to disturb and terrify it, but which in its innermost meaning is a word of peace and harmony. One thinks of chapter twelve of the Fourth Gospel, where the voice that responds to Jesus from heaven is perceived by the crowd as thunder.

In proposing Psalm 29 for the prayer of Lauds, the Liturgy of the Hours invites us to assume an attitude of profound and trusting adoration of the divine Majesty. The biblical cantor takes us to two moments and two places. At the center (vv. 3–9) we have the account of the storm which is unleashed from the "immensity of the waters" of the Mediterranean. In the eyes of biblical man, the sea waters incarnate the chaos which attacks the beauty and splendor of creation, to corrode, destroy and demolish it. So, in observing the storm that rages, one discovers the immense power of God. The one who prays sees the hurricane move north and hammer the mainland. The tall cedars of Lebanon and of Mount Sirion, sometimes called Hermon, are struck by the flashing lightning and seem to jump under the thunderbolts like frightened animals. The crashes draw closer, crossing the entire Holy Land, and move south, to the desert steppes of Kades.

After this picture of strong movement and tension, by contrast, we are invited to contemplate another scene, portrayed at the beginning and the end of the Psalm (vv. 1–2 and 9–11). Distress and fear are now countered by the adoring glorification of God in the temple of Zion.

There is almost a channel of communication that links the sanctuary of Jerusalem and the heavenly sanctuary: in both these sacred places, there is peace and praise is given to the divine glory. The deafening sound of the thunder gives way to the harmony of liturgical singing; terror gives way to the certainty of divine protection. God now appears, "enthroned over the flood" as "King forever" (v. 10), that is as Lord and supreme Sovereign of all creation.

Before these two antithetical scenes, the praying person is invited to have a two-fold experience. First of all he must discover that God's mystery, expressed in the symbol of the storm, cannot be grasped or dominated by man. As the Prophet Isaiah sings, the Lord, like lightning or a storm, bursts into history sowing panic among the perverse and oppressors. With the coming of his judgment, his proud adversaries are uprooted like trees struck by a hurricane or like the cedars shattered by the divine thunderbolts (see Isaiah 14:7–8).

What becomes evident in this light is what a modern thinker (Rudolph Otto) has described as the *tremendum* of God: his ineffable transcendence and presence as a just judge in the history of humanity. The latter is vainly deluded in opposing his sovereign power. In the *Magnificat* Mary was also to exalt this aspect of God's action: "He has shown strength with his arm, he has scattered the proud in the imagination of their hearts; he has put down the mighty from their thrones" (Luke 1:51–52).

However, the Psalm gives us another aspect of God's face, the one that is discovered in the intimacy of prayer and in the celebration of the liturgy. According to the above-mentioned thinker, it is the *fascinosum* of God that is the fascination that emanates from his grace, the mystery of love that is poured out upon the faithful, the serene certainty of the blessing reserved for the just. Even facing the chaos of evil, the storms of history, and the wrath of divine justice itself, the one who prays feels at peace, enfolded in the mantle of protection which Providence offers those who praise God and follow his ways. Through prayer, we learn that the Lord's true desire is to give peace. In the temple, our anxiety is soothed and our terror wiped out; we participate in the heavenly liturgy with all the children of God, angels, and saints. And following the storm, image of the destruction of human malice like the deluge, there now arches in the heavens the rainbow of divine blessing, reminiscent of "the everlasting covenant between God and every living creature of all flesh that is upon the earth" (Genesis 9:16).

The Father's exalted voice resounds at the Son's Baptism blessing the waters of the earth. This message stands out above all in the Christian rereading of the Psalm. If the seven thunders of our Psalm represent God's voice in the cosmos, the loftiest expression of this voice is the one in which the Father, in the theophany of Jesus' Baptism, revealed his deepest identity as the "beloved Son" (Mark 1:11).

POPE INNOCENT III
(1198–1216)

From a sermon on The Feast of the Resurrection

How Abundant Is Your Goodness

O how abundant is your goodness
that you have laid up for those who fear you,
and accomplished for those who take refuge in you,
in the sight of everyone!

PSALM 31:19

SECULAR PEOPLE ARE ABLE to listen but cannot yet hear, since the animal-like person does not perceive those things that are in divine scripture, just as someone may hear a song but does not perceive the melody.

"O how abundant," the Psalmist says, "is your goodness that you have laid up for those who fear you." That goodness is partly tasted already by those who, although in the body on earth, are to some degree already in heaven in the spirit. They say with St. Paul, "Our conversation in heaven" (Philippians 3:20) is that manna hidden (Hebrews 9:4) in the savoring of reading, meditation, and prayer.

79

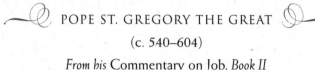

POPE ST. GREGORY THE GREAT
(c. 540–604)

From his Commentary on Job, *Book II*

We Are Led by Steps to the Eternal

For a day in your courts is better
than a thousand elsewhere.

PSALM 84:10A

SINCE HOLY SCRIPTURE SPEAKS to us who are brought forth in time, it is good that it should use words significant of time, in order that it may lift us up by coming down to our understanding. And while Scripture relates something that belongs to eternity, but in the manner of time, it gradually transfers to the eternal world those who are habituated to this world. That eternity, which is unknown, speaks to us with words that we know, and successfully imparts itself to our minds.

What wonder it is, in Holy Scripture, that God isn't overhasty to disclose the unchangeableness of his Nature to the mind of man! After he had celebrated the triumph of his Resurrection, it was by certain steps

80

that God made known the incorruptibility of the body which he resumed again. We have learned from the testimony of St. Luke that he first sent angels to some that were looking for him in the tomb, and then to the disciples who were talking of him along the way that he himself appeared, yet not so as to be known by them. It was after the delay of an exhortation that he showed himself to them in the breaking of bread. At last, entering suddenly, our Lord not only presented himself to be known by sight, but to be handled also.

It was because the disciples still had faint hearts, that in coming to the knowledge of this marvelous mystery they were to be nourished by such a progressive method. Little by little in seeking they might find some portion, so that in finding they might grow, and in growing they might hold faster to the truths they had learned. Similarly, then, we are not led to the eternal world all at once, but by a progression of cases and of words, by slow steps, organized by the One who views even time itself out of time.

POPE PIUS XII
(1939–58)

From the encyclical "On the Mystical Body of Christ"

God Withholds No Good Thing

> *For the LORD God is a sun and shield;*
> *he bestows favor and honor.*
> *No good thing does the LORD withhold*
> *from those who walk uprightly.*

PSALM 84:11

NO ONE . . . CAN DENY that the Holy Spirit of Jesus Christ is the one source of whatever supernatural powers enters into the Church and its members. For "the Lord bestows favor and honor" as the Psalmist says. But that men should persevere constantly in their good works, that they should advance eagerly in grace and virtue, that they should strive earnestly to reach the heights of Christian perfection and at the same time to the best of their power should stimulate others to attain the same goal—all this the heavenly Spirit does not will to effect unless they contribute their daily share of zealous activity. "For divine favors are conferred not on those who sleep, but on those who watch," as St. Ambrose says.

POPE JOHN PAUL II

General Audience, March 26, 2003

Teach Us to Number Our Days Aright

Lord, you have been our dwelling-place
        in all generations.
Before the mountains were brought forth,
        or ever you had formed the earth
        and the world,
        from everlasting to everlasting you are God.

You turn us back to dust,
    and say, "Turn back, you mortals."
For a thousand years in your sight
        are like yesterday when it is past,
        or like a watch in the night.

You sweep them away; they are like a dream,
        like grass that is renewed in the morning;
in the morning it flourishes and is renewed;
        in the evening it fades and withers.

For we are consumed by your anger;
by your wrath we are overwhelmed.
You have set our iniquities before you,
our secret sins in the light of
your countenance.

For all our days pass away under your wrath;
our years come to an end like a sigh.
The days of our life are seventy years,
or perhaps eighty, if we are strong;
even then their span is only toil and trouble;
they are soon gone, and we fly away.

Who considers the power of your anger?
Your wrath is as great as the fear that
is due to you.
So teach us to count our days
that we may gain a wise heart.
PSALM 90:1–12

THE VERSES THAT HAVE JUST echoed in our ears
and in our hearts are a sapiential meditation which,
however, has the tone of a supplication. In fact, in
Psalm 90 the one who prays the Psalm puts at the
heart of his prayer one of the topics most explored

85

by philosophy, most sung by poetry and most felt by human experience in all ages and in all the regions of the earth: human frailty and the passing of time.

It is enough to think of certain unforgettable pages of the Book of Job, which present our frailty. In fact, we are like those who "dwell in houses of clay, whose foundation is in the dust, who are crushed more easily than the moth. Between morning and evening they are destroyed; they perish for ever without anyone regarding it" (Job 4:19–20). Our life on earth is "but a shadow" (Job 8:9). Again, Job continues to confess: "My days are swifter than a runner; they flee away, they see no happiness. They shoot by like skiffs of reed, like an eagle swooping on its prey" (Job 9:25–26).

At the beginning of his song, which is akin to an elegy, the Psalmist insistently contrasts the eternity of God with the fleeting time of humanity. This is his most explicit declaration: "For a thousand years in your sight are but as yesterday when it is past, or as a watch of the night."

As a consequence of original sin, by divine command, man returns to the dust from which he was taken, as already affirmed in the account of Genesis: "You are dust, and to dust you shall return" (Genesis

3:19). The Creator, who shapes the human creature in all his beauty and complexity, is also the One who "turns men back into dust." And "dust" in biblical language is also a symbolic expression for death, the lower regions, the silence of the tomb.

The sense of human limitation is intense in this entreaty. Our existence has the frailty of the grass that springs up at dawn; suddenly it hears the whistle of the sickle that reduces it to a heap of hay. The freshness of life all too soon gives way to the aridity of death.

As often occurs in the Old Testament, the Psalmist associates this radical weakness with sin. In us there is finiteness but also culpability. For this reason, the Lord's anger and judgment seem to overshadow our lives. "Truly we are consumed by your anger, filled with terror by your wrath. Our guilt lies open before you. . . . All our days pass away in your anger." (vv. 7–9)

At the dawn of the new day, with this Psalm, the liturgy of Lauds rouses us from our illusions and our pride. Human life is limited: "Our span is seventy years or eighty for those who are strong," the Psalmist affirms. Moreover the passing of the hours, days, and months is marked by "sorrow and toil" (v. 10) and the years themselves turn out to be like a "sigh" (v. 9).

This, then, is the great lesson: the Lord teaches us to "count our days" so that by accepting them with healthy realism "we may gain wisdom of heart" (v. 12). But the person praying asks something more of God: that his grace support and gladden our days, even while they are so fragile and marked by affliction. May he grant us to taste the flavor of hope, even if the tide of time seems to drag us away. Only the grace of the Lord can give our daily actions consistency and perpetuity: "Let the favor of the Lord our God be upon us: give success to the work of our hands, give success to the work of our hands" (v. 17).

In prayer let us ask God that a reflection of eternity penetrate our brief lives and actions. With the presence of divine grace in us, a light will shine on the passing of our days, misery will be turned into glory, what seems not to make sense will acquire meaning.

Let us conclude our reflection on Psalm 90 by leaving the word to early Christian tradition, which comments on the Psalter having in the background the glorious figure of Christ. Thus for the Christian writer Origen, in his *Treatise on the Book of Psalms* which has been handed down to us in the Latin translation of St. Jerome, the Resurrection of Christ gives us the possibility, perceived by the Psalmist, to "rejoice and be glad all our days" (v. 14). This is because Christ's Paschal Mystery is the source of our life beyond death: "After being gladdened by the Resurrection of Our Lord, through whom we believe we have been redeemed and will also rise one day, we now live in joy the days that remain of our life, exulting because of this confidence, and with hymns and spiritual chants we praise God through Jesus Christ Our Lord" [Origen, *Treatise on the Book of the Psalms*].

POPE JOHN PAUL II

General Audience, July 23, 1986

For he will command his angels concerning you
    to guard you in all your ways.
On their hands they will bear you up,
    so that you will not dash your foot
    against a stone.

PSALM 91;11–12

The Lord has established his
    throne in the heavens,
    and his kingdom rules over all.
Bless the Lord, O you his angels,
    you mighty ones who do his bidding,
    obedient to his spoken word.

PSALM 103;19–20

THE OLD TESTAMENT EMPHASIZES *especially the special participation of the angels* in the celebration of the glory which the creator receives as a tribute of praise on the part of the created world. The Psalms are in a special way the interpreters of this voice, when, for example, they proclaim "Praise the Lord from the heavens, praise him in the heights! Praise him all his angels . . ." (Psalm 148:1–2). Similarly in Psalm 103: "Bless the Lord, O you his angels, you mighty ones who do his word, hearkening to the voice of his word" (v. 20)! This last verse of Psalm 103 indicates that the angels *take part*, in a way proper to themselves, in God's government of creation, as "the mighty ones who do his word" according to the plan established by Divine Providence. To the angels in particular is entrusted a special care and solicitude for people, whose requests and prayers they present to God as, mentioned, for example, in the Book of Tobit (cf. especially Tobit 3:17 and 12:12). Psalm 91 proclaims: "For to his angels he has given command about you . . . upon their hands they shall bear you up, lest you dash your foot against a stone" (vv. 11–12). Following the Book of Daniel it can be said that the tasks of angels as ambassadors of the living God extend not only to individual human beings and to those who have special duties, but also to entire nations (Daniel 10:13–21).

POPE ST. LEO THE GREAT

From a Christmas homily

Happy Are Those Whom You Discipline

Happy are those whom you discipline, O LORD,
and whom you teach out of your law.

PSALM 94:12

THE FACT THAT JESUS CHRIST deigned to become a partaker of our lowliness, and willed to be one of us corruptible, mortal ones, is so sacred and wonderful that the reasons for it cannot be seen by the wisdom of this world. We need the true light that has scattered the darkness of human ignorance. For not only in the work of the virtues, or in the observance of the commandments, but also in the course of faith, hard and narrow is the way that leads to life (Matthew 7:14), and it needs great labor and discernment to walk the one path of sound doctrine without stumbling, and though the snares of error are all around, to avoid all danger of deception.

Who is suited for this, if he is not taught and led by the spirit of God? As the Apostle says, "Now we have received not the spirit of the world, but the Spirit that is from God, so that we may understand the gifts bestowed on us by God" (1 Corinthians 2:12), and King David sings, "Happy are those whom you discipline, O Lord, and whom you teach out of your law." (Psalm 94:12).

General Audience, November 30, 2005

The Lord Frees His People from Bondage

> By the rivers of Babylon—
>> there we sat down and there we wept
>> when we remembered Zion.
> On the willows there
>> we hung up our harps.

PSALM 137:1-2

LET US MEDITATE ON Psalm 137, whose first
words in the Latin version became famous: *Super
flumina Babylonis*. The text evokes the tragedy lived by
the Jewish people during the destruction of Jerusalem
in about 586 BC, and their subsequent and consequent
exile in Babylon. We have before us a national hymn
of sorrow, marked by a curt nostalgia for what has
been lost. This heartfelt invocation to the Lord to
free his faithful from slavery in Babylon also expresses
clearly the sentiments of hope and expectation of
salvation with which we have begun our journey
through Advent.

The background to the first part of the Psalm (vv. 1–4) is the land of exile with its rivers and streams, indeed, the same that irrigated the Babylonian plain to which the Jews had been deported. It is, as it were, a symbolic foreshadowing of the extermination camps to which the Jewish people—in the century we have just left behind us—were taken in an abominable operation of death that continues to be an indelible disgrace in the history of humanity. The second part of the Psalm (vv. 5–6) is instead pervaded by the loving memory of Zion, the city lost but still alive in the exiles' hearts.

The hand, tongue, palate, voice, and tears are included in the Psalmist's words. The hand is indispensable to the harp-player: but it is already paralyzed (see v. 5) by grief, also because the harps are hung up on the poplars. The tongue is essential to the singer, but now it is stuck to the palate (v. 6). In vain do the Babylonian captors "ask . . . for songs . . . , songs . . . of joy" (v. 3). "Zion's songs" are "song[s] of the Lord" (vv. 3–4), not folk songs to be performed. Only through a people's liturgy and freedom can they rise to Heaven. God, who is the ultimate judge of history, will also know how to understand and accept, in accordance with his justice, the cry of victims, over and above the tones of bitterness that sometimes colors them.

Let us entrust ourselves to St. Augustine for a further meditation on our Psalm. The great Father of the Church introduces a surprising and very timely note: he knows that there are also people among the inhabitants of Babylon who are committed to peace and to the good of the community, although they do not share the biblical faith; the hope of the Eternal City to which we aspire is unknown to them. Within them they have a spark of desire for the unknown, for the greater, for the transcendent: for true redemption. And Augustine says that even among the persecutors, among the non-believers, there are people who possess this spark, with a sort of faith or hope, as far as is possible for them in the circumstances in which they live. With this faith, even in an unknown reality, they are truly on their way towards the true Jerusalem, towards Christ.

With this openness of hope, Augustine also warns the "Babylonians"—as he calls them—those who do not know Christ or even God and yet desire the unknown, the eternal, and he warns us too, not to focus merely on the material things of the present but to persevere on the journey to God. It is also only with this greater hope that we will be able to transform this world in the right way. St. Augustine says so in these words: "If we are citizens of Jerusalem . . . and must live in this land, in the confusion of this world and in this Babylon where we do not dwell as citizens but are held prisoner, then we should not just sing what the Psalm says but we should also live it: something that is done with a profound, heartfelt aspiration, a full and religious yearning for the eternal city."

He adds with regard to the "earthly city called Babylon," that it "has in it people who, prompted by love for it, work to guarantee it peace—temporal peace—nourishing in their hearts no other hope, indeed, by placing in this one all their joy, without any other intention. And we see them making every effort to be useful to earthly society."

"Now, if they strive to do these tasks with a pure conscience, God, having predestined them to be citizens of Jerusalem, will not let them perish within Babylon: this is on condition, however, that while living in Babylon, they do not thirst for ambition, short-lived magnificence or vexing arrogance. . . . He sees their enslavement and will show them that other city for which they must truly long and towards which they must direct their every effort."

Let us pray to the Lord that in all of us this desire, this openness to God, will be reawakened, and that even those who do not know Christ may be touched by his love so that we are all together on the pilgrimage to the definitive City, and that the light of this City may appear also in our time and in our world.

POPE LEO XIII

(1878–1903)

From the encyclical "On the Origin of Civil Power"

Sing a New Song

I will sing a new song to you, O God;
  upon a ten-stringed harp I will play to you,
the one who gives victory to kings,
  who rescues his servant David.

PSALM 144:9–10

ALL THINGS THAT ARE OF a civil nature the Church acknowledges and declares to be under the power and authority of the ruler; and in things whereof for different reasons the decision belongs both to the sacred and to the civil power, the Church wishes that there should be harmony between the two so that injurious contests may be avoided. As to what regards the people, the Church has been established for the salvation of all men and has ever loved them as a mother. For it is the Church which by the exercise of her charity has given gentleness to the minds of men, kindness to their manners, and justice to their laws. Never opposed to honest liberty, the Church has always detested a tyrant's rule. This custom . . . is notably expressed by St. Augustine when he says that "the Church teaches kings to study the welfare of their people, and people to submit to their kings, showing what is due to all: and that to all is due charity and to no one injustice."

For these reasons . . . your work will be most useful and salutary if you employ with us every industry and effort which God has given you in order to avert the dangers and evils of human society. Strive with all possible care to make men understand and show forth in their lives what the Catholic Church teaches on government and the duty of obedience. Let the people be frequently urged by your authority and teaching to fly from the forbidden sects, to abhor all conspiracy, to have nothing to do with sedition, and let them understand that they who for God's sake obey their rulers render a reasonable service and a generous obedience. And as it is God "who gives victory to kings" and grants to the people . . . it is to Him that we must pray, beseeching Him to incline all minds to uprightness and truth, to calm angry passions, to restore the long-wished-for tranquility to the world.

POPE JOHN PAUL II

General Audience, February 26, 2003

Music and Hymnody Should Be Worthy of the Greatness of the Liturgy

Praise the LORD!
Praise God in his sanctuary;
  praise him in his mighty firmament!
Praise him for his mighty deeds;
  praise him according to his surpassing
  greatness!

Praise him with trumpet sound;
  praise him with lute and harp!
Praise him with tambourine and dance;
  praise him with strings and pipe!
Praise him with clanging cymbals
  praise him with loud clashing cymbals!
Let everything that breathes praise the LORD!
  Praise the LORD!

PSALM 150

101

PSALM 150, WHICH WE HAVE just proclaimed, rings out for the second time in the *Liturgy of Lauds*: a festive hymn, an alleluia to the rhythm of music. It sets a spiritual seal on the whole Psalter, the book of praise, of song, of the liturgy of Israel.

The text is marvelously simple and transparent. We should just let ourselves be drawn in by the insistent call to praise the Lord: "Praise the Lord . . . praise him . . . praise him!" The Psalm opens presenting God in the two fundamental aspects of his mystery. Certainly, he is transcendent, mysterious, beyond our horizon: his royal abode is the heavenly sanctuary, "his mighty heavens," a fortress that is inaccessible for the human being. Yet he is close to us: he is present in the holy place of Zion and acts in history through his mighty deeds that reveal and enable one to experience "his surpassing greatness" (vv. 1–2).

Thus between heaven and earth a channel of communication is established in which the action of the Lord meets the hymn of praise of the faithful. The liturgy unites the two holy places, the earthly temple and the infinite heavens, God and man, time and eternity.

During the prayer, we accomplish an ascent towards the divine light and together experience a descent of

God who adapts himself to our limitations in order to hear and speak to us, meet us and save us. The Psalmist readily urges us to find help for our praise in the prayerful encounter: sound the musical instruments of the orchestra of the temple of Jerusalem, such as the trumpet, harp, lute, drums, flutes, and cymbals. Moving in procession was also part of the ritual of Jerusalem (see Psalm 118:27). The same appeal echoes in Psalm 47:7: "Sing praise with all your skill!"

Hence, it is necessary to discover and to live constantly the beauty of prayer and of the liturgy. We must pray to God with theologically correct formulas and also in a beautiful and dignified way. In this regard, the Christian community must make an examination of conscience so that the beauty of music and hymnody will return once again to the liturgy. They should purify worship from ugliness of style, from distasteful forms of expression, from uninspired musical texts which are not worthy of the great act that is being celebrated.

The Psalmist ends with an invitation to "every living being" (v. 5), to give praise, literally every breath, everything that breathes, a term that in Hebrew means "every being that breathes," especially every living person. In the divine praise then, first of all, with his heart and voice, the human creature is involved. With him all living beings, all creatures in which there is a breath of life (see Genesis 7:22) are called in spirit, so that they may raise their hymn of thanksgiving to the Creator for the gift of life. Following up on this universal invitation, St. Francis left us his thoughtful "Canticle of Brother Sun," in which he invites us to praise and bless the Lord for all his creatures, reflections of his beauty and goodness.

All the faithful should join in this hymn in a special way, as the Epistle to the Colossians suggests: "Let the Word of Christ dwell in you richly, as you teach and admonish one another in all wisdom, and as you sing psalms and hymns and spiritual songs with thankfulness in your hearts to God" (Colossians 3:16). The highest music is what comes from our hearts. In our liturgies this is the harmony God wants to hear.

PERMISSIONS

SELECTIONS FROM THE WRITINGS of the Holy Fathers that predate World War II are taken from a variety of sources. Most of the selections from the sermons of Pope John Paul II and Pope Benedict XVI, as well as other modern Holy Fathers, are taken from the Vatican's website, and all are used by permission.

INDEXES

A. PSALMS REFERENCED

B. POPES REFERENCED

ABOUT PARACLETE PRESS

Who We Are

Paraclete Press is a publisher of books, recordings, and DVDs on Christian spirituality. Our publishing represents a full expression of Christian belief and practice—from Catholic to Evangelical, from Protestant to Orthodox.

We are the publishing arm of the Community of Jesus, an ecumenical monastic community in the Benedictine tradition. As such, we are uniquely positioned in the marketplace without connection to a large corporation and with informal relationships to many branches and denominations of faith.

What We Are Doing
Books

Paraclete publishes books that show the richness and depth of what it means to be Christian. Although Benedictine spirituality is at the heart of all that we do, we publish books that reflect the Christian experience across many cultures, time periods, and houses of worship. We publish books that nourish the vibrant life of the church and its people—books about spiritual practice, formation, history, ideas, and customs.

We have several different series, including the best-selling Paraclete Essentials, and Paraclete Giants series of classic texts in contemporary English; A Voice from the Monastery—men and women monastics writing about living a spiritual life today; award-winning literary faith fiction and poetry; and the Active Prayer Series that brings creativity and liveliness to any life of prayer.

Recordings

From Gregorian chant to contemporary American choral works, our music recordings celebrate sacred choral music through the centuries. Paraclete distributes the recordings of the internationally acclaimed choir Gloriæ Dei Cantores, praised for their "rapt and fathomless spiritual intensity" by *American Record Guide*, and the Gloriæ Dei Cantores Schola, which specializes in the study and performance of Gregorian chant. Paraclete is also the exclusive North American distributor of the recordings of the Monastic Choir of St. Peter's Abbey in Solesmes, France, long considered to be a leading authority on Gregorian chant.

DVDs

Our DVDs offer spiritual help, healing, and biblical guidance for life issues: grief and loss, marriage, forgiveness, anger management, facing death, and spiritual formation.

Learn more about us at our website:
www.paracletepress.com, or call us toll-free at 1-800-451-5006.

Christmas with the Holy Fathers

$17.95, HARDCOVER
ISBN 978-1-55725-603-4

THERE IS NOTHING MORE BEAUTIFUL than the Christmas season as it is celebrated at St. Peter's Basilica and throughout Vatican City. The dark nights, glowing candles, incense, and music infuse the season with the spirit of God.

This beautiful book shares the Christmas messages—from Advent through Epiphany—given by the Holy Fathers throughout history, from Pope Leo the Great to Pope John Paul II and Pope Benedict XVI.

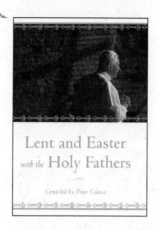

Lent and Easter
with the Holy Fathers

Compiled by Peter Celano

Lent and Easter with the Holy Fathers

$17.99, HARDCOVER
ISBN 978-1-55725-692-8

SPEND THIS LENT AND EASTER in the good company of popes past and present. These reflections, homilies, and special messages from Holy Fathers down through the ages will inspire you toward a good Lent and a joyful Easter!

As Pope Clement XIII said in a 1759 encyclical, Easter is the celebration "by which alone the dignity of all other religious occasions is consecrated."

Available from most booksellers or through Paraclete Press:
www.paracletepress.com • 1-800-451-5006

Try your local bookstore first.